The BIG BOOK of
flute songs

AVAILABLE FOR:
Flute, Clarinet, Alto Sax, Tenor Sax, Trumpet,
Horn, Trombone, Violin, Viola, and Cello

ISBN 978-1-4234-2663-9

HAL•LEONARD®

Visit Hal Leonard Online at
www.halleonard.com

Contact Us:
Hal Leonard
7777 West Bluemound Road
Milwaukee, WI 53213
Email: info@halleonard.com

In Europe contact:
Hal Leonard Europe Limited
Distribution Centre, Newmarket Road
Bury St Edmunds, Suffolk, IP33 3YB
Email: info@halleonardeurope.com

In Australia contact:
Hal Leonard Australia Pty. Ltd.
4 Lentara Court
Cheltenham, Victoria, 3192 Australia
Email: info@halleonard.com.au

CONTENTS

ALL MY LOVING
from A HARD DAY'S NIGHT

FLUTE

Words and Music by JOHN LENNON
and PAUL McCARTNEY

ALL THE SMALL THINGS

Flute

Words and Music by TOM DE LONGE
and MARK HOPPUS

ALLEY CAT

FLUTE

By FRANK BJORN

ANOTHER ONE BITES THE DUST

Flute

Words and Music by
JOHN DEACON

AMERICA
from the Motion Picture THE JAZZ SINGER

Flute

Words and Music by
NEIL DIAMOND

9

ANY DREAM WILL DO

from JOSEPH AND THE AMAZING TECHNICOLOR® DREAMCOAT

Flute

Music by ANDREW LLOYD WEBBER
Lyrics by TIM RICE

BE TRUE TO YOUR SCHOOL

FLUTE

Words and Music by BRIAN WILSON
and MIKE LOVE

BAD DAY

FLUTE

Words and Music by
DANIEL POWTER

BARELY BREATHING

FLUTE

Words and Music by
DUNCAN SHEIK

(It's A)
BEAUTIFUL MORNING

FLUTE

Words and Music by FELIX CAVALIERE
and EDWARD BRIGATI, JR.

BEAUTY AND THE BEAST

from Walt Disney's BEAUTY AND THE BEAST

Flute

Lyrics by HOWARD ASHMAN
Music by ALAN MENKEN

Moderately slow

BEYOND THE SEA

FLUTE

Words and Music by CHARLES TRENET,
ALBERT LASRY and JACK LAWRENCE

BLACKBIRD

FLUTE

Words and Music by JOHN LENNON
and PAUL McCARTNEY

Slowly and smoothly

BLUE SUEDE SHOES

flute

Words and Music by
CARL LEE PERKINS

BOOGIE WOOGIE BUGLE BOY
from BUCK PRIVATES

FLUTE

Words and Music by DON RAYE
and HUGHIE PRINCE

THE BRADY BUNCH

Theme from the Paramount Television Series THE BRADY BUNCH

Flute

Words and Music by SHERWOOD SCHWARTZ
and FRANK DEVOL

BUTTERFLY KISSES

Flute

Words and Music by BOB CARLISLE
and RANDY THOMAS

BREAKING FREE

from the Disney Channel Original Movie HIGH SCHOOL MUSICAL

FLUTE

Words and Music by
JAMIE HOUSTON

25

CABARET
from the Musical CABARET

Flute

Words by FRED EBB
Music by JOHN KANDER

CALIFORNIA DREAMIN'

Flute

Words and Music by JOHN PHILLIPS
and MICHELLE PHILLIPS

CANDLE IN THE WIND

Flute

Words and Music by ELTON JOHN
and BERNIE TAUPIN

CHIM CHIM CHER-EE

from Walt Disney's MARY POPPINS

Flute

Words and Music by RICHARD M. SHERMAN
and ROBERT B. SHERMAN

Lightly, with gusto

small notes optional

CLOCKS

FLUTE

Words and Music by GUY BERRYMAN, JON BUCKLAND,
WILL CHAMPION and CHRIS MARTIN

(They Long to Be)
CLOSE TO YOU

Flute

Lyric by HAL DAVID
Music by BURT BACHARACH

COLORS OF THE WIND
from Walt Disney's POCAHONTAS

Flute

Music by ALAN MENKEN
Lyrics by STEPHEN SCHWARTZ

COME FLY WITH ME

Flute

Words by SAMMY CAHN
Music by JAMES VAN HEUSEN

Moderate Swing

COPACABANA
(At the Copa)
from Barry Manilow's COPACABANA

Flute

Music by BARRY MANILOW
Lyric by BRUCE SUSSMAN and JACK FELDMAN

DO-RE-MI

from THE SOUND OF MUSIC

Flute

Lyrics by OSCAR HAMMERSTEIN II
Music by RICHARD RODGERS

DO WAH DIDDY DIDDY

Flute

Words and Music by JEFF BARRY
and ELLIE GREENWICH

(Sittin' On)
THE DOCK OF THE BAY

FLUTE

Words and Music by STEVE CROPPER
and OTIS REDDING

DON'T BE CRUEL
(To a Heart That's True)

Flute

Words and Music by OTIS BLACKWELL
and ELVIS PRESLEY

DON'T LET THE SUN GO DOWN ON ME

Flute

Words and Music by ELTON JOHN
and BERNIE TAUPIN

DON'T SPEAK

Flute

Words and Music by ERIC STEFANI
and GWEN STEFANI

D.S. al Coda

CODA

small notes optional

DRIFT AWAY

flute

Words and Music by
MENTOR WILLIAMS

DUKE OF EARL

Flute

Words and Music by EARL EDWARDS,
EUGENE DIXON and BERNICE WILLIAMS

THEME FROM E.T. (THE EXTRA-TERRESTRIAL)

from the Universal Picture E.T. (THE EXTRA-TERRESTRIAL)

FLUTE

Music by
JOHN WILLIAMS

EDELWEISS

from THE SOUND OF MUSIC

Flute

Lyrics by OSCAR HAMMERSTEIN II
Music by RICHARD RODGERS

EVERY BREATH YOU TAKE

FLUTE

Music and Lyrics by
STING

EVERYTHING IS BEAUTIFUL

Flute

Words and Music by
RAY STEVENS

Moderately fast

FALLIN'

Flute

Words and Music by
ALICIA KEYS

FIELDS OF GOLD

FLUTE

Music and Lyrics by
STING

FLY LIKE AN EAGLE

Flute

Words and Music by
STEVE MILLER

FOR ONCE IN MY LIFE

Flute

Words by RONALD MILLER
Music by ORLANDO MURDEN

Slowly, with feeling

FOREVER YOUNG

Flute

Words and Music by ROD STEWART,
JIM CREGAN, KEVIN SAVIGAR and BOB DYLAN

FUN, FUN, FUN

Flute

Words and Music by BRIAN WILSON
and MIKE LOVE

THE GIRL FROM IPANEMA
(Garôta de Ipanema)

Flute

Music by ANTONIO CARLOS JOBIM
English Words by NORMAN GIMBEL
Original Words by VINICIUS DE MORAES

GOD BLESS THE U.S.A

FLUTE

Words and Music by
LEE GREENWOOD

GONNA BUILD A MOUNTAIN

from the Musical Production STOP THE WORLD – I WANT TO GET OFF

Flute

Words and Music by LESLIE BRICUSSE
and ANTHONY NEWLEY

GOODBYE YELLOW BRICK ROAD

Flute

Words and Music by ELTON JOHN
and BERNIE TAUPIN

GREEN GREEN GRASS OF HOME

FLUTE

Words and Music by
CURLY PUTMAN

HAPPY DAYS
Theme from the Paramount Television Series HAPPY DAYS

FLUTE

Words by NORMAN GIMBEL
Music by CHARLES FOX

HAVE I TOLD YOU LATELY

Flute

Words and Music by
VAN MORRISON

Slowly, with expression

HEART AND SOUL

from the Paramount Short Subject A SONG IS BORN

Words by FRANK LOESSER
Music by HOAGY CARMICHAEL

Flute

HOGAN'S HEROES MARCH

from the Television Series HOGAN'S HEROES

Flute

By JERRY FIELDING

HERE WITHOUT YOU

Words and Music by MATT ROBERTS,
BRAD ARNOLD, CHRISTOPHER HENDERSON
and ROBERT HARRELL

Flute

I DREAMED A DREAM

from LES MISÉRABLES

Flute

Music by CLAUDE-MICHEL SCHÖNBERG
Lyrics by ALAIN BOUBLIL, JEAN-MARC NATEL
and HERBERT KRETZMER

Music and French Lyrics Copyright © 1980 by Editions Musicales Alain Boublil
English Lyrics Copyright © 1986 by Alain Boublil Music Ltd. (ASCAP)
Mechanical and Publication Rights for the U.S.A. Administered by Alain Boublil Music Ltd. (ASCAP) c/o Spielman Koenigsberg & Parker LLP,
Richard Koenigsberg, 1745 Broadway, New York NY 10019, Tel 212-453-2500, Fax 212-453-2550, ABML@skpny.com
International Copyright Secured. All Rights Reserved. This music is copyright. Photocopying is illegal.
All Performance Rights Restricted.

I HEARD IT THROUGH THE GRAPEVINE

Flute

Words and Music by NORMAN J. WHITFIELD
and BARRETT STRONG

I SAY A LITTLE PRAYER

FLUTE

Lyric by HAL DAVID
Music by BURT BACHARACH

I WHISTLE A HAPPY TUNE

from THE KING AND I

Flute

Lyrics by OSCAR HAMMERSTEIN II
Music by RICHARD RODGERS

I WILL REMEMBER YOU

Theme from THE BROTHERS McMULLEN

Flute

Words and Music by SARAH McLACHLAN,
SEAMUS EGAN and DAVE MERENDA

I WRITE THE SONGS

Flute

Words and Music by
BRUCE JOHNSTON

I'M POPEYE THE SAILOR MAN

Theme from the Paramount Cartoon POPEYE THE SAILOR

Flute

Words and Music by
SAMMY LERNER

IF I EVER LOSE MY FAITH IN YOU

Flute

Music and Lyrics by
STING

IMAGINE

FLUTE

Words and Music by
JOHN LENNON

Medium slow

IT'S MY LIFE

Flute

Words and Music by JON BON JOVI,
RICHARD SAMBORA and MARTIN SANDBERG

Moderately

IT'S STILL ROCK AND ROLL TO ME

Flute

Words and Music by
BILLY JOEL

Moderately fast Rock Shuffle

To Coda

D.C. al Coda

CODA

JAILHOUSE ROCK

Flute

Words and Music by JERRY LEIBER
and MIKE STOLLER

JOY TO THE WORLD

Flute

Words and Music by
HOYT AXTON

Moderate Gospel Rock

JUMP, JIVE AN' WAIL

FLUTE

Words and Music by
LOUIS PRIMA

KANSAS CITY

FLUTE

Words and Music by JERRY LEIBER
and MIKE STOLLER

KOKOMO
from the Motion Picture COCKTAIL

Flute

Words and Music by MIKE LOVE, TERRY MELCHER,
JOHN PHILLIPS and SCOTT McKENZIE

LET 'EM IN

Flute

Words and Music by
PAUL and LINDA McCARTNEY

LET'S STAY TOGETHER

Flute

Words and Music by AL GREEN,
WILLIE MITCHELL and AL JACKSON, JR.

LIKE A ROCK

FLUTE

Words and Music by
BOB SEGER

LIVIN' LA VIDA LOCA

Flute

Words and Music by ROBI ROSA
and DESMOND CHILD

LOVE AND MARRIAGE

Flute

Words by SAMMY CAHN
Music by JAMES VAN HEUSEN

LOVE STORY
Theme from the Paramount Picture LOVE STORY

FLUTE

Music by FRANCIS LAI

MAGGIE MAY

Flute

Words and Music by ROD STEWART
and MARTIN QUITTENTON

MAKING OUR DREAMS COME TRUE
Theme from the Paramount Television Series LAVERNE AND SHIRLEY

Flute

Words by NORMAN GIMBEL
Music by CHARLES FOX

MAYBE I'M AMAZED

Flute

Words and Music by
PAUL McCARTNEY

MICHELLE

FLUTE

Words and Music by JOHN LENNON
and PAUL McCARTNEY

MICKEY MOUSE MARCH

from Walt Disney's THE MICKEY MOUSE CLUB

Flute

Words and Music by
JIMMIE DODD

MISSION: IMPOSSIBLE THEME

From the Paramount Television Series MISSION: IMPOSSIBLE

FLUTE

By LALO SCHIFRIN

MISTER SANDMAN

FLUTE

Lyric and Music by
PAT BALLARD

MOON RIVER

from the Paramount Picture BREAKFAST AT TIFFANY'S

FLUTE

Words by JOHNNY MERCER
Music by HENRY MANCINI

MY HEART WILL GO ON
(Love Theme from 'Titanic')
from the Paramount and Twentieth Century Fox Motion Picture TITANIC

Flute

Music by JAMES HORNER
Lyric by WILL JENNINGS

MY WAY

Flute

English Words by PAUL ANKA
Original French Words by GILLES THIBAULT
Music by JACQUES REVAUX and CLAUDE FRANCOIS

NA NA HEY HEY KISS HIM GOODBYE

Flute

Words and Music by ARTHUR FRASHUER DALE,
PAUL ROGER LEKA and GARY CARLA

ON BROADWAY

FLUTE

Words and Music by BARRY MANN,
CYNTHIA WEIL, MIKE STOLLER and JERRY LEIBER

PEPPERMINT TWIST

Flute

Words and Music by JOSEPH DiNICOLA
and HENRY GLOVER

POCKETFUL OF MIRACLES

FLUTE

Words by SAMMY CAHN
Music by JAMES VAN HEUSEN

Moderately, with a lilt

PUFF THE MAGIC DRAGON

Flute

Words and Music by LENNY LIPTON
and PETER YARROW

PUT YOUR HAND IN THE HAND

FLUTE

Words and Music by
GENE MacLELLAN

QUIET NIGHTS OF QUIET STARS
(Corcovado)

Flute

English Words by GENE LEES
Original Words and Music by ANTONIO CARLOS JOBIM

Moderately slow

ROCK AROUND THE CLOCK

FLUTE

Words and Music by MAX C. FREEDMAN
and JIMMY DeKNIGHT

ROCK WITH YOU

Flute

Words and Music by
ROD TEMPERTON

Moderate Rock

SATIN DOLL

Flute

By DUKE ELLINGTON

SAVE THE BEST FOR LAST

Flute

Words and Music by PHIL GALDSTON, JON LIND and WENDY WALDMAN

THEME FROM "SCHINDLER'S LIST"

from the Universal Motion Picture SCHINDLER'S LIST

Flute

Music by JOHN WILLIAMS

SHE WILL BE LOVED

Flute

Words and Music by ADAM LEVINE
and JAMES VALENTINE

Moderately

To Coda

D.S. al Coda

CODA

Play 3 times

SING

from SESAME STREET

Flute

Words and Music by
JOE RAPOSO

Moderately

SO LONG, FAREWELL
from THE SOUND OF MUSIC

Flute

Lyrics by OSCAR HAMMERSTEIN II
Music by RICHARD RODGERS

SOMEWHERE OUT THERE
from AN AMERICAN TAIL

Flute

Music by BARRY MANN and JAMES HORNER
Lyric by CYNTHIA WEIL

SPANISH FLEA

FLUTE

Words and Music by
JULIUS WECHTER

STACY'S MOM

FLUTE

Words and Music by CHRIS COLLINGWOOD
and ADAM SCHLESINGER

Medium Rock

SUNRISE, SUNSET
from the Musical FIDDLER ON THE ROOF

Flute

Words by SHELDON HARNICK
Music by JERRY BOCK

Moderately slow Waltz tempo

TAKE MY BREATH AWAY
(Love Theme)
from the Paramount Picture TOP GUN

Flute

Words and Music by GIORGIO MORODER
and TOM WHITLOCK

THAT'S AMORÉ
(That's Love)
from the Paramount Picture THE CADDY

Flute

Words by JACK BROOKS
Music by HARRY WARREN

THIS LAND IS YOUR LAND

Flute

Words and Music by
WOODY GUTHRIE

Moderately bright

THOSE WERE THE DAYS

Flute

Words and Music by
GENE RASKIN

TIME AFTER TIME

Flute

Words and Music by CYNDI LAUPER
and ROB HYMAN

A THOUSAND MILES

Flute

Words and Music by
VANESSA CARLTON

Moderately fast

small notes optional

To Coda

TOMORROW
from the Musical Production ANNIE

Flute

Lyric by MARTIN CHARNIN
Music by CHARLES STROUSE

Moderately slow

TOP OF THE WORLD

Flute

Words and Music by JOHN BETTIS
and RICHARD CARPENTER

TWIST AND SHOUT

Flute

Words and Music by BERT RUSSELL
and PHIL MEDLEY

UNCHAINED MELODY

FLUTE

Lyric by HY ZARET
Music by ALEX NORTH

UNDER THE BOARDWALK

Flute

Words and Music by ARTIE RESNICK
and KENNY YOUNG

Moderately, with a beat

UNITED WE STAND

Flute

Words and Music by ANTHONY TOBY HILLER
and JOHN GOODISON

THE WAY YOU MOVE

flute

Words and Music by ANTWAN PATTON,
PATRICK BROWN and CARLTON MAHONE

WE ARE THE WORLD

Flute

Words and Music by LIONEL RICHIE
and MICHAEL JACKSON

WE BELONG TOGETHER

Flute

Words and Music by MARIAH CAREY,
JERMAINE DUPRI, MANUEL SEAL, JOHNTA AUSTIN,
DARNELL BRISTOL, KENNETH EDMONDS, SIDNEY JOHNSON,
PATRICK MOTEN, BOBBY WOMACK and SANDRA SULLY

Slow Soul

WHAT THE WORLD NEEDS NOW IS LOVE

Flute

Lyric by HAL DAVID
Music by BURT BACHARACH

WITH A LITTLE HELP FROM MY FRIENDS

Flute

Words and Music by JOHN LENNON
and PAUL McCARTNEY

WONDERFUL TONIGHT

FLUTE

Words and Music by
ERIC CLAPTON

WOOLY BULLY

Flute

YELLOW SUBMARINE

Flute

Words and Music by JOHN LENNON
and PAUL McCARTNEY

YOU ARE THE SUNSHINE OF MY LIFE

Flute

Words and Music by
STEVIE WONDER

YOU RAISE ME UP

Flute

Words and Music by BRENDAN GRAHAM
and ROLF LOVLAND

Moderately slow

small notes optional

YOU'VE GOT A FRIEND

Flute

Words and Music by
CAROLE KING

ZIP-A-DEE-DOO-DAH

from Walt Disney's SONG OF THE SOUTH
from Disneyland and Walt Disney World's SPLASH MOUNTAIN

Words by RAY GILBERT
Music by ALLIE WRUBEL

Flute